# FEEL GOOD
# NAKED

# FEEL GOOD NAKED

## 35 Secrets Of Irresistible Body Confidence

Ana Wilde

# Love From Ana.com

# Contents

# FEEL GOOD ABOUT YOURSELF

"Feel Good Naked" is all about having confidence in yourself and feeling great in intimate situations.

If the thought of getting naked in front of a guy (any guy) sometimes puts you off the whole idea of sex (or even dating), it's time to learn how to love your naked body – exactly how it is.

That's right, you don't have to change yourself in any way to love yourself. You are lovable exactly as you are, and any changes and "improvements" you make are just icing on the cake of the beautiful body you already have.

Don't believe me?

Stick with me through this book and you will!

Although many women are not as confident as they would like to be, even when dressed, wearing clothes at least gives some measure of comfort. You have a shield between you and the world. But confidence can disappear entirely when it is time to get naked. Suddenly you are expected not only to reveal all, but also to make sure he has a good time. And if that wasn't enough, you're supposed to enjoy the whole experience too (or at least to look as if you are to avoid denting his ego).

**2**

If you hate displaying your body in all its glory, getting intimate with your guy becomes very stressful.

Understandably you may feel nervous about appearing naked in front of a guy you like. You feel exposed and vulnerable. It can be excruciating with a new guy, but many women go through life only making love with the lights off, even with a guy they have been with for years.

When you feel happy with your body, sex becomes a much more enjoyable experience. You have fewer inhibitions. Your confidence in yourself shows and helps your guy to relax too. Those positive vibes you give out make him view you as more desirable than someone who has a poor opinion of herself and her body and is reluctant to reveal all and let go. Confidence in bed beats having a perfect body every time.

"Feel Good Naked" is designed to help you feel more comfortable with your naked body and to feel more comfortable with sex in general. It is the second book in the "Captivating Confidence" series of books that are all about having rock solid self-esteem — a level of confidence in yourself that is so attractive to others.

This book is a natural follow-on from the first book in the series, "You Are Beautiful! 53 Easy Ways To Love Your Imperfect Self" You may not need to read book one if you feel reasonably happy with how you look and only lack confidence when it comes to peeling off your clothes. On the other hand, you can never have too much confidence either fully dressed or naked!

However you feel about yourself right now, don't worry, there's a way forward. We're going to take this one step at a time and build up your confidence so that you can enjoy every moment with your guy.

By implementing the ideas in this book, you can expect to

- feel sexier and more attractive

- understand how to relax and enjoy sex more than you ever have before

- worry less about what he is thinking in bed

- accept the gorgeous, sexual side of you that you may have been too self-conscious to reveal in the past

- have altogether more confidence in yourself.

So, let's begin.

# How To Use This Book

"Feel Good Naked" includes 35 key confidence-boosting strategies. Please don't try to do them all at once. You'll get much further much faster by taking things a few steps at a time.

Begin by reading through the whole book. It's designed to be practical and deliberately short so you can quickly get started on your "feel good naked" mission.

Pick two or three strategies that resonate most with you, and play with those ideas in your mind. Put them into practice, see them working and then pick one or two more. That way, you will enjoy an almost instant boost to your confidence and see results right away to give you the motivation to continue.

You absolutely don't have to work through all of the strategies. If one or two strategies don't appeal or don't apply to you, feel free to leave them and pick something else. Just be aware that it is sometimes the strategies that you are most resistant to, the ones you instantly dismiss, that you need the most.  But you can always come back to them later and review how you feel about them.

By working through the book a few steps at a time in this way, you'll have a personal plan for increasing your confidence in bed in the shortest possible time.  You will love feeling more confident about yourself!

# WAIT! A Gift For You!

Would you like more confidence in all parts of your life?

Do you want to feel better about yourself in every way?

"Feel Good Naked" focuses on feeling great about revealing your body in intimate situations. But if you are generally low in self-esteem, your lack of confidence can affect every area of your life, including your career, your relationships and your happiness now and in the future.

As a thank you for taking a look at "Feel Good Naked", you can answer one quick survey question about confidence and download a FREE e-copy of my book "How To Be Confident And Happy With Yourself" (which is out in paperback priced at $9.99).

This book is a step-by-step guide to having more general confidence in your life, and if you couple that with the strategies in this book, your confidence really will sky-rocket.

Visit the link below to take the one-question survey and get your FREE book today!

http://lovefromana.com/moreconfidence

Now let's really get started.

# 1

# Realize How Much Of You Is Already A Turn On

If you talk to guys, you might be amazed at the things they find lovable about the women they sleep with that you don't even think about.

You spend your time worrying they will be turned off by a few extra pounds or the nose you hate or whatever else you decide is less than perfect about you, and they are lusting after all sorts of things about you that you never imagined.

You have a head start because guys love all this about you:

- Your Softness - your skin, your hair, your body is much softer than his. He loves that.

- Your Scent - whether you wear a light fragrance or not, you have a natural scent that turns him on.

- Your Femininity - the very fact you are female, with characteristics that are very different to him, gives you a huge boost in the attraction stakes!

- Your Enthusiasm - if you enjoy making love to him, that's very attractive. A reluctant lover who has to be cajoled into sex is much less so. But there's no point in getting naked unless you really want to be there, so enthusiasm is an attribute you should have in bucketfuls!

- Your Curves - no matter how "uncurvy" or "over-curvy" you feel, you are more curvy than him and he loves every one of them.

- Your Sensuality - he loves how much you enjoy using your senses to eat, to listen to music, to touch him etc even before you get to bed, and then your sensuality can keep him enthralled between the sheets.

- Your Kisses - he will be turned on by your kisses if he wants to sleep with you.

- Your Smile - he loves when you smile at him and your smile reaches your eyes.

- Your Hair - long or short, it's another aspect of your femininity he adores.

- Your Erogenous Zones - he loves turning you on and especially all those little places he doesn't have.

Remember all these things that men love about you when you start giving yourself a hard time for not being attractive enough.

# 2

# Discover Your Gorgeousness

I can hear you protesting at this point. Somehow you don't feel gorgeous. Or perhaps you're thinking I am going to tell you to find your good points and play them up. You can do that. Of course, you can. But your gorgeousness is so much more than that.

Your gorgeousness is the essence of you. It's not just about being beautiful on the inside, advice that has been doled out to girls who think they look ugly since cave girl refused to come out in case cave guy spotted her on a bad hair day. But feeling beautiful inside is part of it.

It's not your lovely personality that he reacts to in bed (though that may be what makes him want to be your guy). He wants to be with you, for sure. But it's the whole fact that you are a woman, the very femaleness of you, that attracts him.

You may not think you are very feminine for various reasons. Perhaps you have a flat chest or you feel big and ungainly, rather than petite. But you can be sure that you are female through and through, and you are a lot more female than he is!

However feminine you feel, it doesn't matter. You are all woman. Your body, your hormones, your sex is female. Your very scent is designed to attract him and keep him interested – it doesn't matter what your shape is. It's about your female essence and that's the gorgeousness that he reacts to in bed.

If you want to feel more attractive than you do right now, play up your feminine qualities. That does not mean that we are all the same and have to look like Stepford wives – femaleness comes in many forms.

What words do we associate with the female of the species? Here is a selection. You might be able to think of more. Look down the list. Take on board any of these characteristics that already apply to you, and own them - embrace them. Remember, you do not have to change to feel better, you only have to accept that you are already attractive. Changing can be the icing on the cake if you like. Accepting is what counts right now and is all up to you. It's all in your head!

So here are those qualities that are seen as being more feminine than masculine:

- gamine
- elfin
- petite
- soft
- bouncy
- bountiful
- fecund
- rounded
- curvaceous
- shy
- diffident
- smooth
- cuddly
- smiling
- ladylike

- elegant
- womanly
- girly
- motherly
- tender
- warm
- compassionate
- shapely
- voluptuous
- ample
- buxom
- kindhearted
- friendly
- flirty
- chatty
- tactile
- delicate
- welcoming
- helpful
- sympathetic
- affectionate

- genial
- amicable
- zany
- romantic

I'm not trying to be sexist here. It's not that guys can't be some of those things - for example, affectionate or romantic. But if you pictured a person with any one of those characteristics, you would generally picture a woman rather than a man. Just compare arrogant, conceited, masterful, dominant, angry, hard, solid, stout, hairy, bearded, rough or strong and you picture a man, don't you? So don't over-think this. Just claim the female words that apply to you.

When I say embrace and own those terms, you can just mull them over and fully accept that they apply to you, or you can emphasize those aspects of you so that you feel more and more like that.

You could let those parts of your personality come to the foreground, especially when you are with your guy or when you are relaxing. (They will not be appropriate everywhere. For example, you don't want to start becoming girly and flirtatious if you work in banking and want to be taken seriously!)

If you want to feel more feminine, you can easily wear clothes that both play up those traits and flatter your figure. You can match any of the traits you want to own with an outfit or just start wearing more feminine clothes in general. Just be sure to choose only those clothes that suit the type of woman you are and your body shape. A gamine Audrey Hepburn style is different from a floaty, floral-loving romantic, for example.

Clothes that make you feel more feminine will still make you feel that way when you take them off. Try wearing skirts and dresses rather than trousers, capris and leggings rather than jeans, blouses and tops rather than shirts, embellished and shaped tops and t-shirts rather than plain styles or slogans.

And don't forget sexy lingerie.

Though you believe that your body is not made for it, there is sexy lingerie to suit EVERY body shape, whether boyish or buxom. Boyish shapes suit simple styles in feminine colors with very little embellishment. Try little shorts with delicate lace edging and thigh-high stockings, plus a little camisole. More buxom figures suit well-constructed undies with boning and good stitching and are made for a basque or corset. That may not be something you want to wear every day, but on a special date, his eyes will pop out when he sees you. I defy you not to feel sexy in a well-fitting basque.

But what does the wearing of clothes have to do with feeling good about your naked body?

After all, you're going to take them all off, aren't you?

That's true. But they are another way of reinforcing good thoughts about yourself. If you look good in public, if you move freely, if you are able to express your sense of style fully clothed, then you will have more confidence in being you in bed.

This means you can practice enjoying how you look all day long, and your guy will get a sense of the real you, happy in your skin, before you get anywhere near the bedroom. And that means you are already sexy before you peel off a single thing.

# 3

# Appreciate Your Sexy Self

Once you have discovered your gorgeousness from Strategy 2, make sure you take the time to appreciate it. Once you have worked out the essential female qualities you have decided to "own", write them down in a list.

And add to that all those things he likes about you from Strategy 1.

But there's even more to appreciate. Add anything you like about your face, your body and your hair. There is always something that you overlook unless you consider each little part of you. Perhaps you like your delicate ears that are so sensitive when he kisses them, your beautiful shoulders, your expressive eyes, your knees.

And appreciate those parts of you that let you be a sexy woman in bed, for example, your arms that hold him tight, your hands and fingers that touch and stroke, your thighs that wrap around him and turn him on, your sensitive nipples.

You get the idea. Remember, your sexy self is not a two-dimensional picture he's looking at and criticizing. You're a whole living, breathing sexual being who he's having fun with. He's not looking for faults because he's enjoying being with you.

# 4

# Don't Worry About Comparisons

We are all subjected to pictures of perfect women all the time in the media. Magazines and movies would have us believe that cellulite doesn't exist, bottoms are always petite yet rounded and breasts defy gravity and are full and pert.

Your confidence can easily falter if you compare your own body and its flaws with those perfect women, even though common sense tells you that those images have been enhanced with air-brushing and clever camera angles.

We know real women are not perfect. We see women in the street and they are not perfect. Our friends are not perfect and we love them anyway.

But we also know that he sees those pictures in the media and watches those movies too. Will he be expecting your body to look like that? Will he be measuring you against the impossible yardstick of those models and celebrities?

Set your mind at rest.

Guys don't make comparisons like that. They see "a beautiful woman" in an image. They see "a beautiful woman" in their bed. It would not cross their minds to compare the two and say, "Hey you, get out of my bed because you have a muffin top and ample bottom and that picture I saw of Kylie in that magazine you left open on the coffee table doesn't."

He understands that magazines print pictures of beautiful girls. But he doesn't look for Kylie in his bed. He's happy with you. He's not thinking you are second best because you have cellulite on your thighs. Cellulite is not even on his radar. Enjoy that he doesn't give a stuffed fig that you're not perfect. You may not look as good as Kylie in a bodycon dress, but you can still look beautiful and have confidence in bed.

If you're worried about being perfect like a celebrity, remember that you are the one he is with - not that perfect celebrity - and he will love to see you lost in passion in a way he will never see those models and movie stars. He loves looking at you, because you are with him in the moment, and he is happy you are there.

# 5

# Work Up To Nakedness

Avoiding sex is not the answer if you lack confidence in your body. Of course, it removes the problem temporarily, but all it really does is create a barrier in your mind, and you'll get more and more worried about revealing all.

The best thing to do with fears is to face them. If you want to have sex, and this is the only thing standing in your way, you will confuse your guy with the mixed signals you are sending out.

In any case, you don't have to get naked right away.

There's no need to peel off every stitch like a striptease artist and parade around the room. It can be just as exciting to leave some clothes on.

You don't have to wear the kind of crotchless undies you get in sex shops to turn your guy on. Keep that until you know him well and what he likes!

A silky, sexy slip can cover the bits you're concerned about and still keep him happy. High heels are a turn on for a lot of guys and make your legs look longer and slimmer. And a corset will flatten your tummy and lift your boobs. You can even make love in just a dress shirt or a skirt and nothing else. It adds to the fun and might leave you less self-conscious.

One trick if you're particularly worried about being naked with a new guy is to get him all riled up outside the bedroom.

Spend plenty of time making out and getting friendly before going further. Show him what a hot kisser you are, plant kisses down his body, fondle each other through your clothes.

Let him see him how sexy you are with your clothes on, and you'll know just how much he likes you and your body before you get naked. You may be so worked up yourself at that point that you just won't care how you look.

You can take this one step further and actually make love fully or partially clothed in the car, in the kitchen, on the sofa, the first time.

If you do that, there will be less awkwardness when you actually go to bed and get naked with him. You already know how much he appreciates what you can do for him, and hopefully you'll be so eager to experience what he can do for you that you won't care about him seeing you. Things can only get hotter.

Being able to see you naked in action improves the experience for him. Guys love the visual aspect of sex, even if you'd prefer to stay covered. You'll find him even more heated up when he can see the whole of you, and therefore the sexier you will feel.

## Undress Slowly

You may to tempted to get the evil moment when you have to appear naked over with and throw off all your clothes as fast as possible before hiding under the sheets, but you will seem more confident and turn him on more if you shed each layer slowly and make the act of getting undressed part of your foreplay. That way, it's not a sudden jarring view of your naked body in all its glory but a slow sensual buildup.

# 6

# Be In The Know

Rather than worrying about how you look when you are in bed with a guy, aim to ensure you both enjoy the experience.

To do this, you have to know what you like as well as what gives him pleasure.

For your own part, you need a measure of self-awareness so that you know exactly what buttons to press, and what turns you on. Without that knowledge, it will be hard to get lost in the moment.

Spend some time on your own, in your room, your bed or the shower, enjoying your body and experiencing how much pleasure you can give yourself with no guy in sight. This is a good investment of your time. Not only can you find out exactly what your body is capable of in terms of pleasure (multiple orgasms anyone?), but it will also show you another way to see and accept how sexy you are.

For this exercise, don't use a vibrator, unless you are going to introduce one into bed with your guy. Even then, it is good to know how to manually stimulate yourself to orgasm so that you're not always relying on toys.

It's often said that guys are pretty selfish lovers, but actually most guys love to see you climax. The fact that they can make you happy in bed gives them a sense of power and pride which feeds their ego.

But men are not mind readers, and most, especially less experienced lovers, would love you to gently guide their hand, fingers or lips, or say, "I love it when you...", telling them whatever floats your boat. Unfortunately, if you don't know what gets you over the edge, you can't show him what works.

Knowing you can take your body to the heights of pleasure is something else to be proud of. And all it takes is practice. We are all capable of masturbating to orgasm. He is not going to care about extra pounds or lack of them here and there when you show him what a sexy lady you are.

As for pleasing him, if you have a sexy trick or two in your repertoire to delight your guy, it can do great things for your confidence.

Do you know how to turn a guy on? If you know how to give your guy a great time in bed and that he will be back begging for more, it can take the worry right out of being naked.

This book is not a sex manual, but if you don't know how to be good in bed, it's worth investing in your education.

Spend some time reading or watching educational videos so you are not in the dark about what lovers do to pleasure each other.

It really is in your power to give immense delight to a man, so why have that chunk of your education missing, or feel uncertain about what to do in bed, when you don't need to remain ignorant? You might think that everyone knows what to do naturally or finds out from whispered conversations with friends, but it's not always the case even in this day and age. Educate yourself, and you'll feel much more confident.

Although education is a good thing, you don't have to take on board everything you read. Remember, it's all about your pleasure too.

Don't try to be too wild in bed if you are inexperienced. A few basic moves can go a long way and will be easier to manage if you are starting out. You can add to your repertoire over time.

He might even freak out if you come over all porn star on the first night together. On the other hand he might just like it – play it by ear! Learn what guys like in general, and then find out through experience what your guy likes in particular (as every guy is different).

If you focus on enjoying yourself and making sure he does too and let everything else just fade away, you won't be thinking about how your body looks.

Meanwhile, add your sexy skills to the list of things you love about you.

Remember, it doesn't really matter how beautiful or clever or funny you are once you're in bed. If you have a good time with the guy and give him a good time, he'll think you're amazing.

# 7

# Be Into It 100%

One trick when you're in bed with your guy is to be into the whole thing one hundred percent. Right from when things heat up and you decide that getting naked is on the cards, forget everything but giving (and receiving) every jot of pleasure you can. Make it your aim that you both have the best time of your lives.

Don't aim for a big orgasm, like it is the only thing that counts. Get totally lost in the moment so that you only think about what you're actually doing. That means if you're kissing, you're not thinking about what comes next, you're just totally enjoying the kiss.

Guys love enthusiasm and participation. If you find yourself thinking about how you look, about whether your tummy is wobbling or your breasts are drooping, quickly switch your mind to the sensations you are giving or receiving. Get fully into the flow. It's a kind of mindful sex where you only focus on pleasure, and it's ideal for forgetting all about your body. If all else fails, focus your mind on the parts of you that are all about receiving pleasure – your erogenous zones, wherever they are, but in particular your nipples and vaginal area.

Remember, no one looks as pretty as a picture in the throes of orgasm. You may screw up your eyes or open them wide. You may shudder and blush. You may grunt and groan. You will have hair so messed up it looks like it's never seen a hairstylist, dryer or straightener. But no matter, he will think you are the sexiest female ever because he was able to give you that pleasure and make you look that messed up. He loves that look!

# 8

# Be Natural

The less natural you are, the more worried you're going to be about revealing all in bed.

Of course, every women has a few tricks up her sleeve when making the most of herself. We have uplifting and padded bras, undies that squeeze the fat within an inch of its life, false eyelashes and hair extensions. And then there's makeup, and lots of us are never seen in public without it.

When all that comes off (or rubs off on the pillow), there's only you and him though.

Do guys know we have all these tricks?

Of course they do!

Will he be disappointed when he sees the real you, devoid of your "extras"? It's unlikely, unless you have done a real camouflage job. He just wants to get his hands on the real thing. He's not going to be too picky about what you did to get him there.

It's more a case of what is happening in your mind that strikes a blow to your confidence if you are not as natural as you could be.

If you have the chance, try gradually introducing the real you before you end up between the sheets. If you do that, there's no shock factor. Or just avoid extremes of camouflage so your look is a fairly natural one, while still emphasizing your good points.

For example, you can emphasize your eyes with makeup if you like, but don't go over the top with heavy liner, multicolored eye shadow and three coats of mascara. Get used to the beauty of your eyes devoid of too much gunk. That way, you won't have transferred your whole look to the pillow slip by the morning, look like a raccoon and give him a

**34**

fright at the difference in you with and without your eye makeup. You also won't have to worry about that scenario and can just focus on having a good time.

Another example, if you wear padded bras, try lightly padded ones rather than those that make you look two sizes bigger with gel and air pumps or whatever, so that you don't feel worried about looking more petite than he expects when you bare all. You already know he likes the petite look before you get together.

# 9

# Get Used To Being Naked

If the only time you are ever naked is in the shower or when you're having sex, it's time to get used to your body – how it looks and how it feels to be naked.

Take every opportunity you can to be naked while you're alone. Walk around your bedroom when you're getting ready, observe yourself in the mirror, and put your clothes on at the last possible moment.

Sleep naked all the time, not just when he is with you. Get used to the feel of the sheets against your skin and how sensuous that is. Get accustomed to yourself naked and how beautiful it feels not to be constricted by clothes.

Don't just look at your body. Take time to feel your limbs, the lovely rounded shape of your butt and tummy, the smoothness of your skin, the weight of your breasts, the way your nipples react to being touched, and continue to explore yourself. You are not just a look. You are a three-dimensional woman, perfectly fine, erotic and ripe for sex.

If you have plenty of privacy, you can spend the whole day naked at home.

If you're feeling daring and you'd like to experience this, try sunbathing topless or in the nude where it's allowed or if you have an area at home that is not overlooked.

For a cheeky way to get used to being naked, venture out wearing a dress or skirt with no undies every now and again, and feel the air against your skin. If you try this out on a date with your regular partner, see how he reacts when you tell him you're commando. Hot sex is guaranteed, and no worries about how you look...

# 10

# Be Realistic

When you look at real women in the street, how many perfect bodies do you see?

Not many!

There are women of all shapes and sizes – some small, some tall, some fat, some thin, some with small boobs, some with large, some with narrow hips, some with the wide child-bearing kind. Women with real, less-than-perfect bodies are having sex with guys all the time. They are getting married. They are having babies. If having to have a perfect body was an obstacle to getting together with a guy, the human population would die out. And no doubt, every one of those women is also full of insecurity about her naked body.

Is there any need to feel like that?

None whatsoever! It's a real shame taking the joy out of sex, and it's unjustified and unnecessary.

Your real body is just fine like it is. Decide right now that you're going to enjoy it and all the pleasure it brings you, rather than criticize it.

Also have realistic expectations when it comes to sex.

In the same way that magazines and their celebrities can make you think there's something wrong with how you look, romance novels and steamy movies can make you think there's something wrong with your sexual performance.

They never portray the funny bits where your legs won't quite go where they are supposed to in the heat of the moment, nor do they ever show the wobbly bits we all have, or the rude noises we sometimes make. But real sex is not like a movie. Don't let your romantic vision of how you think things should be cloud the good things going on in your life. If you're both enjoying sex as a couple, you're doing it right. That's it.

That's not to say you can't get better at it. The first time with a guy is probably not going to be the best, but over time, as you find out each other's needs and desires, things will improve. And they'll continue to improve over the years if you keep trying new things and have an open mind. So expect things to become brilliant (if they are not already) as long as you are open with each other and willing to say what you want and like.

Remember also to put sex into perspective. Sex is just one of the things you share with a guy. It's not the only thing that counts.

If you're in a relationship with him, he enjoys your company, he finds you attractive and he sees a future with you. You have time to develop your relationship in bed. You don't have to impress him with every move in the Kama Sutra from day one.

And every time doesn't have to be a roaring success. In fact, you learn as much from things that don't work as the things that do about what is right for you both as long as you take it in the spirit of learning together.

The only thing that really matters is that you continue to give each other pleasure and you enjoy your time together overall. The answer is just to relax into it and enjoy the moment. It's not really about what you look like, what he looks like, what you do, what he does. What's important is that you're two people getting it on, having fun.

# 11

# Love Each Little Bit Of You

It's time to give the parts of you that you don't like very much some extra special love and attention.

Every few days take one part of you and gaze at it in the mirror with love and compassion. This is your chance to send love to every scar, ever bulge, every perceived imperfection that you have ever worried about.

Focus on that one part of you all day. Think about how your body created it, what it does for you, how it feels, not just how it looks. You may think this exercise is a bit silly, but it is surprisingly effective.

Remember, scars and stretch marks show our history, what we have been through and come out the other side. Birthmarks are a unique part of us that no one else has. Our rounded bellies are simply the outer cover for the whole wonderful working that goes on beneath the surface. They are soft and squishy and welcoming to those we choose to hug.

Instead of berating yourself about a part of your body you normally find fault with, show some compassion for yourself, and give that part of you some tender loving care with kind thoughts, lotion and massage.

This exercise will help if you find it difficult to love your whole body in one go. Lavish attention on one less loved part at a time, and include more and more parts of you until you love and feel good about your whole self.

# 12

# Enjoy What Your Body Can Do

Remember that your body is not just a picture. You're a living, breathing woman. To appreciate the whole of you, be aware of what your body does for you, not just how it looks.

There are many simple pleasures that your body allows you to enjoy that you may not think about very often. But it truly is wonderful that you can use it to walk, run, dance, swim, and for any other physical movement you're capable of. You can use it show love when you hug a child or kiss and caress a lover. And while you get busy with your day, your body is quietly doing all it can to keep you alive.

If you are used to thinking of your body as something to hate and criticize, it's time to start thinking of it as something to appreciate. You are a high spec wonder of natural engineering, not an ornament.

To help you feel good in bed, be happy about all your body does for you, be amazed at how it works and think about how much pleasure it is capable of between the sheets. If it's not something you've thought about before, spend some time exploring your own body. Learn to give yourself pleasure and fully appreciate what it can do for you.

Then remember how much pleasure you can give to your guy, and you'll realize why how you look is not an issue at all.

Do you think that he worries about your muffin top when you're riding him? Nothing could be further from his mind, believe me! In bed, it's not all about your shape, it's skin against skin and all those fantastic sensations he's feeling. He's not getting that from any picture of a supermodel.

# 13

# Does Everyone Look Like This?

We all know how other women look fully clothed, but very few of us outside the medical profession are familiar with how women look naked. Don't worry that your body's more intimate areas are abnormal from catching a glimpse of a few pictures here and there.

Just as we all have different faces, we all have different looks when it comes to the vaginal area too, but we have the same basic features – outer lips (or labia), inner lips, vagina and clitoris, plus the area between the vagina and anus called the perineum and then the anus itself. It's a pretty sure thing that you are normal down there.

However they look, your lady parts are pretty attractive to a guy. Don't worry, he is never going to turn his nose up at you because you have an ugly set! There's no such thing.

You may be nervous about whether you should shave or wax the hair down there, but that is a purely personal decision. Most women like to trim and neaten the hair so that it looks neat in a bikini or undies, but there's no need to go completely bare unless you want to. In porn pictures and movies, you will see that most woman go bare or have a little patch of hair, but that is just so that the cameras get a better view.

Some guys like a bare look and others like a bit of fur. You may want to take his views into account if you care about that, but feel free to ignore them too – it's your vagina after all! Are you insisting he gets waxed? Maybe you should if he is so particular!

The other thing that women worry about is odor. If you are clean and healthy, there is nothing unpleasant about the smell from your vaginal region, but if you think it is strong and unpleasant and you have any kind of discharge, see your doctor.

The normal smell of your vagina is a big turn on for your guy so don't try and disguise it with vaginal deodorants and perfumed soap.

As you get more aroused, the smell will become slightly stronger and become even more of a turn on. Be proud of your feminine aroma and how wet you get when you are turned on. It's very sexy and shows that you are into what you are doing and not just going through the motions to keep him happy.

# 14

# Take Care Who You Sleep With

There are guys who will love you just the way you are and want to be your boyfriend. There are husbands who will say their vows and really mean them. Then there are players and serially unfaithful guys.

A player or unfaithful husband can easily destroy your confidence, make you feel that you are not good enough for him and that you are to blame for him not wanting you, when really it is just the type of guy he is. It would not matter what you looked like or how you were in bed, he would be playing the field.

Just look at those beautiful celebrities you admire so much. Do they have boyfriends and husbands who are unfaithful? They do – nearly every one! It's not about you and how you look, it's about what is going on in the guy's head or, more likely, his pants!

If you are the confident type, you can sleep with a string of guys (if that is what you want to do) and not care whether you see them again. In this day and age, there's no stigma in that.

But if you are shy and are seeking reassurance that you are attractive, a lot of first or second dates ending up in sex or one night stands won't help you one bit. They will make you feel worse. Yes, you will feel attractive enough to get lots of guys into bed. Most of them will be happy to bed you, but if they are not sticking around (and many won't), that can be quite demoralizing.

If you are sensitive enough to worry about what you look like in bed, don't open your heart (or your legs) until you are happy the guy is into you and not just into any woman who will sleep with him.

Work on feeling attractive in your own right. You don't need to have your attractiveness validated by guys wanting to sleep with you. You are worth someone special who wants to stay with you.

There is a theory that you inevitably attract the people who reflect the thoughts you have about yourself. The more self-worth you have, the better the guys you attract.

The slimeballs and douche bags look for girls with low self-esteem as they will more easily fall prey to their techniques. They don't bother with those who know their own high value because they can't manipulate these women. Confident girls see through the tricks and tactics.

If you are constantly having your confidence undermined by your choice of partners, it's time to stop and see what is happening. Build yourself up and choose one of the good guys.

The more sex you have with your guy (the decent kind), the more confidence you'll gain in your body, in the pleasure you can give and receive, and you'll know for sure that you're attractive – not only to the one in bed with you but also to yourself.

# 15

# How To Deal With
# A Critical Guy

Your long-term partner might throw the odd teasing comment about how you have put on weight or are showing a few gray hairs. It can be hurtful, but he's not trying to hurt you, as a rule. Tell him it upsets you when he says these things, even if they are true. Tell him you're trying to build up your confidence, and he's not helping.

If your guy is constantly critical of you, it may be because you've never told him to stop. Teasing can easily get out of hand. Tell him how hurtful it is, and ask him not to do it any more. If he doesn't stop, then the ball is in your court to decide whether you put up with it. This is a form of bullying and verbal abuse that you can do without.

Some guys just can't help themselves when they use criticism to hurt you. They are deliberately cruel because they are deeply angry inside or emotionally damaged.

If your guy has emotional issues and uses this kind of toxic criticism to take his problems out on you, he needs to get help from a therapist so that he can relate to you in a healthier way. Alternatively suggest couples counseling or just get yourself out of the relationship.

If you don't, he will destroy your self-confidence, and no guy is worth the pain of losing every drop of self-worth you have managed to build up. A trial separation may make him think twice about what he is losing.

There's a particular form of criticism that's very hurtful to hear from a long-term partner, and that's when he says he doesn't find you attractive any more.

Look at what is behind the words because they are often not the full story. Have you actually let yourself go so much that you have changed completely from the woman he found attractive at first? It's unlikely that you were absolutely gorgeous one minute and like an old hag the next, but if you have been letting your standards drop, it does no harm to start caring more about how you look. See if it helps. It will definitely make you feel better about yourself. But don't be perturbed if all your efforts make no difference.

Don't let it destroy your confidence. Many women are tempted to rush out and find a guy (any guy) who does find them attractive, to block out their partner's hateful words. Others stick with their relationship through thick and thin and resign themselves to a sexless future. Neither is necessary. There are often other issues behind this.

When guys go off sex for one reason or another, they often blame their partner to avoid feeling bad about themselves. It's a guy thing. They feel they should be ready for sex at all times, and if they are not, it causes a big dent in their ego.

Going off sex can happen for any number of reasons, and this is not the place to explore them all, but it may be that your guy has been under a lot of stress or pressure at work and that is reducing his libido. He may be suffering from depression and not feeling like sex with you for that reason. If that is the case, then these issues need to be dealt with to get your love life back on track.

**54**

Your guy may even be having an affair and using your looks as an excuse to avoid getting intimate with you. If you suspect this is the case, don't ignore the issue. This will continue to undermine your confidence until you get to the bottom of it.

On the other hand, don't immediately suspect the worst. A surprising number of guys with erectile or ejaculation problems avoid sex and blame their partners rather than admit they have a problem. Could that be the case with your guy?

Persuade your guy to have a full health check, especially if he is showing other signs of ill health. Did you know that erectile problems are often one of the first signs of a potential heart attack? The blood vessels in the penis get furred up along with those around the heart.

In any case, even if it's just that your guy is getting older, there is so much that can be done and still so much fun to be had in bed that it's a shame not to tackle the problem. You need to get him to do something about the issue and visit a medical specialist, not sweep things under the carpet.

That's difficult to do while he's in denial, but if this is the problem you have probably seen the signs already. Let's just say that if you're in bed about to have sex and he is having problems, it most certainly isn't that you're not attractive enough. He doesn't suddenly get turned off after wanting sex with you because he catches sight of an extra bulge, wrinkle or gray hair here or there.

Build up your confidence in other ways while you're having problems, and also find new ways to be close and pleasure each other that don't involve full intercourse. It's time to expand your repertoire, not time to bring your sex life to a close.

# 16

# Get Your Guy On Your Side

If you have a long-term partner, tell him that you'd like to be more confident in bed. He might wonder what you have in mind! Just say that sometimes you feel shy about appearing naked in front of him but that you'd like to get over it so that you feel better about trying new things. He's bound to be keen.

Ask him to remind you of all the things he finds sexy about you. You might be surprised at the things he comes up with. You can also do the same for him and make him feel good too. Make sure he knows that he doesn't have to think up a whole list on the spot when you talk to him or to make things up just to please you. In some ways it's nicer if he gives you compliments at the time, whenever he thinks nice things about you. He may need gentle reminders to do this now and again.

Also ask your guy to tell you what feels good in bed. Couples often don't talk about sex, but if you get over your shyness and do this, you will know what to do more of to keep him happy and where to focus on improving your skills so that you feel like the sexy partner you are.

# 17

# Shut Up About It

All the world over, women are moaning to their men folk about the size of their thighs. Guys are totally bewildered by this.

They hate these conversations and never know what they are supposed to say. If they say, "Yes, your thighs are getting a bit chunky," you'll be all offended. If they say that your thighs look fine to them, you'll think they are being less than honest with you. Guys can't win. It's enough to make them want to cry into their beer.

Really all they want is for your magnificent thighs to be naked and wrapped around them. Whatever size they are, he loves them in bed with him. Just go with his opinion and not yours for once, and don't spoil a good thing by complaining about yourself.

If you do too much complaining about your body, he might start looking more closely and think you have a good point. Every guy wants a good-looking woman on his arm. If you keep telling him what's wrong with you, maybe he'll start to believe you and doubt the attraction he feels for you.

Make it a rule NEVER to go on about your body to him, ever. Act as if you are a beautiful woman, and you will remain one in his eyes.

In fact, acting as if you are a beautiful woman is a good policy all round – a kind of fake it until you make it – or in this case – fake it until you feel it.

The more you act as if you are gorgeous and one sexy beast in bed, the more gorgeous you will be in his eyes. The more you see his admiration and lust reflected back at you, the sexier and more beautiful you will feel. What a happy virtuous (rather than vicious) circle that is.

If you can't seem to get it into your head that you are gorgeous, practice just thinking it by getting lost in the moment every time you have sex, and before long you will feel more gorgeous and sexy than ever.

# 18

# Be Good To You

Do you treat yourself and your body as well as you could?

This book, for the most part, is not so much about changing how you look but about accepting yourself. You are sexy just as you are, and you can enjoy your time in bed with your guy no matter how you look. But it does no harm (and it can do your confidence a lot of good) if you take care of yourself and your health.

Although being good to you includes eating well and taking exercise, it doesn't mean going all out on some mad diet or exercise kick and punishing your body into submission. You can feel and look good without knocking yourself out 24 hours a day or losing half your body weight. You can't achieve perfection, and you should never aim for that. You don't need starvation diets, cosmetic surgery or liposuction, just a healthy regard for you and your body and what makes it feel, as well as look, good.

Eat healthy food most of the time, and don't go wild with booze, cigarettes or anything else that's harmful to you. Keeping yourself healthy always has a knock-on effect on your confidence. In any case, no one ever feels sexy with a hangover, the flu or a mouth that tastes like an old ashtray!

If you think your lack of confidence is due to real issues with your body size and not just about giving yourself a hard time over the extra pounds you carry, it may make you feel better to get yourself in shape. But always make that effort from a position of loving yourself rather than hating your body.

And don't focus solely on your weight. Eat healthily and take some exercise because it makes you feel good, rather than just because you want to lose weight. Try to make a habit of those things you'd be happy to continue forever, rather than going on a strict diet. Also, work on your general confidence at the same time so you are not just relying on losing weight to feel good in bed. As we have seen, there is much more to it than that.

Above all, don't put your life on hold until you feel better about yourself. There's no reason why you can't feel better about yourself right now.

What if you never lose weight? Are you going to be hanging around forever hating yourself? No, stop wishing everything were different and love the you that you are now.

Strike phrases like, "If only I were thinner, I'd be happy to take off my clothes and enjoy sex" and its close cousin, "I'll be happy to go to bed when I lose all this weight" from your vocabulary and out of your mind.

There's no harm in trying to achieve a healthier weight. Just don't hate yourself while you get there. It's counterproductive because you'll need all the encouragement you can get to achieve your goal.

# 19

# Do What Makes You Feel Sexier

There are many who say you should forget trying to look good to be attractive to men, grow the hair on your legs, stop wearing makeup and high heels, and love yourself anyway.

And I totally agree that you should not be forced into improving yourself to conform to anyone else's idea of beauty.

But what if you just feel sexier looking a certain way? What if you want to wear makeup and get rid of the hair from your legs, under your arms and around your bikini line?

Why not do it if it makes you feel better?

I know I feel sexier with fuzz-free legs, with newly washed hair and a touch of makeup, and I don't think there's a woman alive who doesn't want to preen herself a bit for her guy. Even your guy is likely to shower, shave and wear a touch of aftershave for a date with you. It would be rude not to bother at all. It shows a lack of respect for your partner.

As long as you don't get caught in the trap that you are ugly because your body doesn't look a certain way, it's a good thing. Making the effort can help you feel sexier, whatever your shape and size, so I am all for this type of improvement. Being "well presented" or "showing yourself in your best possible light" is not a bad aim and definitely makes you feel more confident.

Here are the things you could do last minute to feel sexier when you get naked:

- Avoid stuffing your stomach with high-carbohydrate foods the day of a date as it's hard even for skinny girls to hide a tummy full of pasta (not that you really need to care, but you'll feel better).

- Pamper your skin so you are soft, without rough patches, and get rid of unwanted hair.

- Keep your hair healthy, soft and touchable, rather than gelled and sprayed to within an inch of its life. The idea is that he can run his hands through it without getting stuck in a nest of styling products.

- Get rid of the rough edges from your nails as well as chipped polish. No one wants their important little places handled by jagged or dirty-looking nails.

- Brush your teeth so they are gleaming and your breath is fresh.

- Add a touch of light fragrance if you like it, but don't overpower him with strong perfume or too many scents from competing products such as shower gel, body lotion and perfume. Use everything from the same range, if you can, to avoid a toxic mix.

Grooming is an area where a little basic maintenance goes a long way. You don't need to live at the beauty salon. If nothing else, just make sure you are clean and fresh and you look after your skin, hair and nails with a few simple routines.

This shows a healthy, balanced attitude to yourself and how you look that translates well to how you feel about yourself in bed.

It's the little touches that can make all the difference when you are naked - clean well-manicured nails versus scratchy, bitten ones, smooth soft skin on your arms versus rough flaky skin, and the fresh scent of you after sexual exertion versus the stale smell of sweat from the grueling day you just had.

It's worth a bit of effort if it makes you feel more attractive and more confident.

# 20

# Take Care Of Your Environment

I don't mean recycling your packaging and avoiding waste (although you should do that too). I mean preparing for sex by setting the stage.

It's difficult to feel confident if you are surrounded by dirty dishes and crumpled sheets and all the outfits you tried on for your date with him are piled up on the bed. Do what you can to prepare, not just you, but also the room, for sex before you get anywhere near that point. If you create a relaxed, sensual atmosphere in the bedroom, you will get into the mood and enjoy the whole experience much more.

Make sure there are soft, clean sheets on the bed and that the room is tidy. Have flowers, oil, soft music, condoms – anything you think might help or you might need (or would like to try!) – on hand without having to scrabble around looking for them. And give the rest of your home a quick clean too. Most guys don't really care (or notice), but you will probably feel better and more relaxed.

No one looks their best under harsh overhead lighting, but making love in the dark is not great for a guy either. It's much better if you have visual cues as to what is turning each of you on. So compromise. Soft lighting from lamps or candlelight will make the bedroom feel more seductive and cast you (and your guy) in the best light.

If you're staying at his place, ask if he has any candles or switch on a lamp rather than the overhead light to keep you both in the mood.

Just be careful that candles can't be knocked over or set fire to anything – the only fire you want going on is between the two of you.

# 21

# Think The Right Thoughts

Whatever thoughts you have about yourself over and over again become ingrained in your brain. Your habitual thoughts gets reflected in your attitude to yourself, as well as in the way you behave. Your thoughts, in effect, create your reality.

That's a scary idea when you are busy thinking you're fat or you're old or you're not fit to be seen naked in bed or "Who would want you anyway?"

But it's also a positive thing because it means you can change everything with the power of your thoughts. And it's not some "woo woo" idea. It has repeatedly been shown in research that our thoughts affect our beliefs which affect our actions which then affect our whole lives.

So, where you are today and what you think about yourself is the result of what you have been thinking about over many years. Your lack of confidence may have started with criticism you received as a child and been strengthened by teasing or bullying you suffered at school, combined with any bad thoughts you have had consistently about yourself.

But it doesn't mean you are stuck where you are.

The best thing you can do is train yourself, through constant repetition and practice, to think the thoughts that are consistent with the woman you want to be. So if you want to be confident, sexy and hot in bed, think only those thoughts that lead you to believe that. And by the same token, squash any thought that you are not the woman you want to be as soon as it drifts into your head.

Remind yourself of your positive characteristics and sexy skills whenever negative thoughts crop up. The more you do it, the better you'll get at this exercise. Before you know it, you will feel confident, sexy and hot. You might think that anything that happens only in your head cannot work that kind of magic, but you just have to try it to believe it.

Incidentally, you can use this not just to increase your confidence in bed but also to improve your self-image in every part of your life. There's no reason why you have to limit your improvements in self-esteem to the bedroom.

# 22

# Get Over Your Fear
# Of Rejection

Fear of rejection is one of the most prevalent of human fears and can be a biggie when you are getting into bed with a guy, especially if it's the first time with him.

But don't forget that he has exactly the same fear, so you have something in common.

Are you about to reject him as soon as he takes off his shirt and pants and peels down his boxers? I thought not. But he thinks you might. Maybe he thinks he's too hairy or his penis is too small, or he's worried he doesn't have a six pack to turn you on.

Does he go on about it or try and hide away with the light off?

No! He just gets on with it.

He knows who he is going to bed with. He already has a good idea what you look like without clothes, unless you have been wearing a tent! He's just dying to feast his eyes on you and enjoy your body. Criticizing you and sending you home is the last thing on his mind.

Beauty really is in the eye of the beholder. Your guy desires you. You are beautiful. Enjoy it. When he's in bed, he's enjoying getting turned on by you. He's thinking, "Wow! I'm getting laid", "I feel really good", "I'm so turned on, I'd better not come too quickly". If he's focusing on your body at all, he's focusing on how much he likes it naked with him.

Fear and desire cancel each other out, so if you want to get rid of your fear, work on raising your desire. This means only making out with guys who you really want to sleep with and not going straight from kissing to sex. Plenty of active foreplay before you reach the bed is a good antidote to fear.

# 23

## Put Legs On Your Table

Although you can do all of the exercises here to build your confidence in bed, there is nothing like a positive experience between the sheets to help make you feel better about yourself in sexual situations - but don't worry about having to get your legs on the table, this is an entirely different kind of strategy!

You can only get so far by reading this book. It's by actually getting into bed and enjoying sex without inhibition that you will put your confidence on more solid ground. To feel how desirable you are and increase your confidence, look at how good sex can be with practice and how much enjoyment you can give to your partner.

You just have to plunge in and build up your confidence as you go, gathering evidence that you are the sexy woman you want to be.

It was Tony Robbins I first heard describe how we can view building a positive image of ourselves (however we want it to be) as putting legs on a table. You just have to decide the picture you want of yourself – that's the table that needs support – and then collect every shred of evidence you can find that it is true – these are the legs to support the belief you want. A table with just a few legs is not too stable and can be toppled with a little push, an unkind remark or a look you decide is a bit off. But a table with a lot of legs will hold up under a lot of pressure, just like a firm belief.

So look for the evidence that you are the woman you want to be

- every time you make love and he finds you sexy

- every time you use one of your sexy skills

- from every part of your body that you know is sexy

- with every wolf whistle or admiring glance that you receive

- every time you look in the mirror and think you're a fine woman (you should be thinking that often by now)every time a guy wants to go to bed with you, whether you accept the invitation or not

- whenever a guy asks you out on a date or for a dance.

You're one sexy woman!

And keep adding legs – never stop. You never know when someone might try and take the legs out from under you, whether with jealous ,bitchy remarks from other women or an off-the-cuff comment from some buffoon in a wine bar. The more legs you have, the less vulnerable you are to having your confidence undermined.

# 24

# Playtime

Making love is not a serious pursuit, so make sure you don't treat it like one. It's playtime for adults and should be fun.

When kids play, they are not self-conscious about their bodies. They revel in how much they can do. You hear them in playgrounds everywhere squealing, "Look! I can climb high! I can run! I can jump!" They are full of delight.

That's exactly how you want to be in bed. No, I don't mean climbing and running and jumping, unless you are extremely athletic and your guy is too! I don't even mean playing sexy games (though that's not a bad idea later down the line). I mean savoring the whole joyful experience of it, taking maximum delight from what you can do with your bodies to pleasure each other.

How would your attitude to sex change if you decided you were just going to have fun and play next time you go to bed with your guy? It's sure to be more fun than worrying about your body, that's for sure.

# 25

# Imagine Your Way To Confidence In Bed

Your imagination can be a great ally when it comes to building your confidence. The thing is your subconscious mind can't tell the difference between your imagination and reality so you can easily have yourself believe whatever you like.

To do this, see yourself in bed in your mind's eye being the 'femme fatale', sex siren or whoever you want to be. Don't imagine you have a different body. Just see yourself exactly as you are in appearance, while being sexy with your man and full of confidence between the sheets.

Imagining how you want to be acts as a kind of mental rehearsal for the real thing so that the situation will seem more familiar and within your comfort zone when you get there. (For the same reason, it's important not to see yourself as a timid mouse in bed, frightened to take your clothes off and reveal all, as that will stop you being a sex goddess in the making!)

To boost your confidence, make the image as vivid as possible in your mind. Don't just picture how you look, think about the sounds you're making, what you're saying, what he's saying and how everything feels. The more details and emotion you inject into this the better.

This is great foreplay that you can do on and off all day long if you know you are likely to end up in bed later. By the time you get together in the evening, you'll be raring to go and will not care about taking your clothes off at all!

If you have already had fun in bed with your guy but you just weren't as confident as you'd like to have been, you can use your "successes" from that time to help build confidence for the future. Recall everything positive that happened, and superimpose upon it a feeling of being on top of world and of having supreme confidence in your ability to turn him on.

If you have had less successful times in bed, take a moment to run through those scenes again. Project in your mind how it could turn out differently with your "new found" confidence as you enjoy displaying your body and skills to give him the time of his life.

Flood your mind with pictures of the "reality" that you want to experience so there is no room left for doubt about your ability to achieve it.

At the end of your time imagining these positive scenarios, see yourself curled up in his arms, both of you happy and satisfied.

If you find this exercise difficult, don't worry, it does get easier with practice. Just try a few minutes here and there, and like everything else you practice consistently, your skill in using your imagination will improve. It's a great way to fill in time when you're waiting in line at the bank or store or getting the bus to work - although you may find people wondering what you're smiling about.

# 26

# Seduce Him

Confidence in bed is often not as much about how you look as how sexy you feel.

One way to feel sexier is by taking on the role of seductress, rather than passively letting things happen. It's something to try once you're feeling a little more confident in yourself in the bedroom.

You may have to act as if you have confidence when you're playing this role until you see it working, but take it slowly to start with, and you will be fine.

If your guy takes the initiative most of the time when it comes to sex, playing the seductress will make him think you are the sexiest woman on the planet, and that will boost your feeling of desirability no end.

To play this role, you simply have to make it clear that you want and desire him. Make him feel good, and it will make you feel good too.

If you lack confidence, don't try this with someone you're not sure of. Most guys prefer to be the ones doing the chasing in a new relationship (whatever they say about wanting to be asked out). Try it on a guy you've been sleeping with for a while.

You can play your seduction game without being too direct if you wish. Flirt with him, tease him gently in an admiring way, or use words with suggestive double meanings. Gaze into his eyes and smile, touch him frequently on the hands, arms or shoulders, rub his wrist gently and whisper into his ear.

You can do this anywhere with a partner you're sure of, even when you're not about to have sex – standing in line for the movie, on your way out to work, at the restaurant waiting for the wine list. He'll think you're hotter than July – but more importantly you will feel it too. Just be ready to actually have sex later in the day, otherwise you're just teasing.

If you have the nerve, and you're getting the right signals back from him, tell him how much you want him. And see just how much he wants you back – a lot!

One note of caution: pay attention to his mood before you get into full seduction mode. Flirt a little and see if he's up for it before you go further. It's a myth that men are ALWAYS ready for sex – sometimes they are not in the mood, too tired or just too stressed out. Pick your moment and watch his reactions and you will usually get the desired result.

Rejection won't help your confidence, but if you do go all out and are rejected, remember that it was most probably just bad timing and not that he thinks you are the monster from the deep.

# 27

# Be Sensual

If you feel good about your own sensuality, it can help you feel sexier in bed and out. Use this feeling in the whole seduction process to help him see you as sexier too.

Sensuality simply means that you are aware of all your senses and enjoy all the sensations that come to you in everyday life. Take time to appreciate everything:

- the beauty of the things that surround you, including color, texture, shape, and how things look as a whole, for example, a beautiful painting, a well-designed room or a rack full of colored scarves

- the flavors in delicious food you eat, from the subtle spices and flavors you detect in new dishes to fine wines and good chocolate

- the aroma of coffee brewing, freshly laundered clothes, the scent of a baby

- good music and the ambient sound of waves or birdsong

- the feel of velvet, flower petals and rough brick

Practice doing everything more sensually. For example, you can eat sensually showing that you are savoring every morsel, walk sensually as if you are feeling the air as you move through it and the clothes against your skin, and talk more sensually as if you are enjoying the sound of the words as they come out of your mouth.

Get the idea that you are a sensual, sexy, desirable woman all day long. He won't be able to resist you.

Then when you are in bed, use your heightened senses to focus on and appreciate everything, from the feel of his hands to the scent of his hair and the sounds you each make.

When you do this, you are lost in your senses and your own pleasure and will lose the self-consciousness that you might otherwise suffer from.

# 28

## Relax

Sexually confident women are relaxed in bed so anything you do that helps you relax will make you feel better.

### Alcohol

You may find a glass of wine relaxes you, and having a drink over dinner is a nice preamble to sex. Just don't go over the top with alcohol or get dependent on it. It's not flattering if you have to be drunk to be relaxed enough to have sex with him.

## Massage

If you feel a little stressed out, ask your partner to give you a massage. This can help ease the way into sex. Even a good neck and shoulder message can make you relax enough to feel turned on.

## Clear The Decks

Make sure you're not worrying about anything when you go to bed as that can severely hamper your enjoyment and ability to lose yourself in the pleasure of it all. A few sex sessions which you don't enjoy can start affecting your confidence as a sexual woman.

Letting anxiety or the size of your "To Do" list ruin your sex life is not going to make you feel good. Do the best you can to clear the decks of things you have on your plate before you go to bed, and then set aside those things you didn't get to and stop worrying about everything.

If you are living with your guy and doing more than your fair share, don't get resentful and worn out. Ask your partner to take on some of the load. He may be keen to help if you explain why you want him to do this.

## Relaxation Techniques

Most people have some degree of worry and stress that can't be easily swept aside, so you may need to learn how to relax to be able to enjoy sex fully. Mastering a relaxation technique will help you in all kinds of situations, not just in bed, so it's well worth doing.

Yoga is one solution. It's a great way to explore how your body feels by getting more in touch with yourself and loving how every part of you works. If you practice regularly, you will also tone and strengthen your muscles, which is no bad thing, and you will become more supple, enabling you to get into the more tricky positions. And because yoga is done in a calm, slow way with long, deep breaths, you learn to relax and reduce stress, all of which help confidence in bed and out.

# 29

# Be Open

If you think about the body language of someone who is not confident, you'll recognize it's all about being protective, closed and contained - arms crossed over the body, looking down rather than out at the world. It's the same in bed. The more open you are and the less you try to hide away, the more confident you'll appear, the more turned on he'll get and the better you'll feel over time.

## Use Open Body Language

Resist the temptation to try and cover yourself once you're naked. It's not the moment to cross your legs and arms to try and keep everything he wants to see hidden from view! The more at ease you seem with being on display, the more sexually confident you'll appear, and the better you'll feel because you'll see how much he likes looking at you. If you never show him, you'll never find out!

## Stretch Out On The Bed

One great way to display yourself is to stretch out like a sex kitten in bed. Lie flat with your arms over your head, like you feel really good being in bed with him. This is something you can do while you're watching him undress. This move not only makes you seem confident and sexy, it also flattens your tummy, lifts your breasts and says, "come and get me" in the nicest possible way.

## Open Up To Him

As he starts to kiss and caress you in bed, tilt your head and upper body back so that he can easily access your throat, collarbone and breasts. As things heat up, you'll naturally feel like opening your legs – don't resist the urge!

# 30

# Don't Be Afraid To Be Vulnerable

We all feel more confident with people and in situations and places that we are used to. You can choose to stay small and keep your world restricted to what you know, or you can choose to expand and become comfortable with new things. Your confidence can't help but increase when you choose to step outside your comfort zone.

When you first start dating, getting into relationships and having sex, it's all new and well outside those things you are familiar with. So don't expect to feel comfortable from day one. Every new relationship means getting used to a different person and becoming familiar with him.

To have a good time in bed with a guy, you have to be willing to step outside your comfort zone a little. Even in a long-term relationship, you need to get comfortable with showing yourself in the throes of passion – something that you will not show to everyone. But then sex is all about getting over yourself – your serious, career-planning, work-mode self and bringing in the wicked, alive, carefree side of you that you don't let everyone see.

It's perfectly okay to be vulnerable. That's one of those feminine qualities he can't help but like about you. Your guy wants to see the real you, and you don't have to pretend you're someone you're not. The more open you are, the more he will appreciate that you are putting your trust in him. This makes it all the more important that you choose the right kind of guy (see Strategy 14).

Acting as if you're confident is great, but quiet confidence is fine. Don't go so overboard that you seem like a fake. He wants to sleep with you, not some figure from fiction – unless it's a game you're both playing. A little bit of play acting is a good thing to help avoid seeming too timid and unsure you want to be there (when you do), but it's also okay to say that you've never tried something before or you're a bit nervous about a new move as long as you are not hiding yourself away through fear.

If you're imagining being someone else to give yourself sexual confidence, make it someone you (and he) could easily imagine you being – just a more sexually confident version of you, not a complete about face into a dominatrix bitch, unless that is who you really are!

# 31

# Take The "Shoulds" & "Should Nots" Out Of Sex

## Be Genuine

Never feel under any kind of obligation to sleep with a guy. There are no circumstances EVER where obligation even exists. Whatever his expectations are, no matter how many dates you have had, no matter how much he pleads and tries to get you into bed out of guilt, the only reason to actually sleep with him is because you want to and because it's right for you.

It's not going to help your confidence in the moment or for future encounters if you don't want to be there.

The fact that you genuinely want to be with a guy shows in your eyes and in your smile. It makes everything about you more attractive. And you feel more attractive.

Want to be there or don't do it. Enough said about that.

## Guilt Free

Give up any feelings of shame you have about enjoying sex. They don't belong in your bedroom or in your life.

Many women feel it's less than ladylike to love sex or show they love it. But it's natural to like sex. It's a way to show him how much of a woman you are. If he's got his head screwed on right, he won't think less of you for loving sex - it will just be one of the things he loves about you. And if he doesn't approve, he needs to change his attitude and get with the twenty-first century not you!

Depriving your guy of the pleasure of seeing you naked and turned on is not kind or loving. Every guy wants to feel skilled in bed, and it's only by knowing he makes you happy between the sheets that he feels good about himself as a lover.

Do your guy a kindness. This does not mean pretending to enjoy it. It means actually enjoying it – having the time of your life – and letting him know that by how you look, the sounds that come out of your mouth and the moves that you make. You need to get over yourself so that you not only enjoy sex when he initiates it but by initiating it too.

## What's Normal?

There's really no such thing as normal when it comes to sexual activity. Everyone has their likes and dislikes and varies in when they first had sex and how many sexual partners they have had. You may be curious and read surveys in women's magazines, but it doesn't really matter where you fit into an average so don't let your past affect your confidence. It doesn't matter at all. Whatever you like in bed and whatever happens to your body when you're turned on, you can be sure you're normal. It's all good. You can never be too turned on or too loud or too wet.

## Trying New Things

Though there are fashions in sex as there are in all things, don't feel that just because you hear about something you should do it. Sex is one of those things where you have to trust your own mind about what will give you pleasure and what you would like to try, but also about what you would find a total turn off.

Keeping an open mind is a good thing. You will not know what you like until you try it, but it doesn't mean that you have to experiment with things where the very thought turns your stomach. That is not going to make you feel good. Confidence is not built by being persuaded to do things against your wishes.

Feel free to say "Yes" or "No" to anything. But there's no need to make your guy feel bad for suggesting something (everyone has their turn ons and their limits). You are turning down the request ("I don't think I'd enjoy that"), not the person.

Simply take responsibility for having the kind of sex you want to have, like the adult you are, and enjoy it. Some guys have expectations they have picked up from looking at porn about what they think women like and are always ready for, but it doesn't mean you have to act like a porn star to fit in with anything he wants.

It may be you who would like to try something new. Be ready to make requests for those things you would like to experience. Do it in the right spirit, that is with the idea you want to experiment a bit. You're not saying he's not satisfying you with what he's done so far. Ask in the firm expectation that he will say "Yes." He most likely will. Most guys are only too happy if you want to explore all the options.

If he says "No," you can handle it. It's not the end of the world. He doesn't want to try something sexually, at least not right at this moment. He's not rejecting you.

You may have shocked him. So what? That's his problem, not yours. You're okay. You're still an incredible person. He just said "No," that's all. If whatever you asked for is within the bounds of sex between consenting adults, you can be sure it's enjoyed by hordes of people around the world, even if it's not something your guy wants to try.

The main thing to get from all this is that you are responsible for your own pleasure. Even though books and magazines talk about guys giving you an orgasm, all he can really do is help you along if you show him the way. A lot of the pleasure is in your head. Confidence in bed means recognizing that and owning the things that you like without shame.

# 32

# Pick Your Position

As I said before, no one looks their best in the throes of orgasm, and whatever position you're in, he's not spending his time pointing out your figure flaws. But if you are sensitive about a particular part of your body, you might feel more relaxed (while you work on your confidence in other ways) with one of the sexual positions which minimizes the view he has of your least favorite feature.

**Doggy style** where you are on all fours and he enters you from behind is good if you're sensitive about your tummy as he'll only have a good view of your back, thighs and butt. He'll love this view especially if you push out your buttocks a little and arch your back. Facing away from him means you won't be tempted to pull in your stomach muscles all the time so you can relax into the position and you might reach orgasm more readily, especially if he or you apply some manual stimulation to your clitoris at the same time.

In the **girl on top** position (sometimes called the cowgirl), you straddle your partner and face him resting on your calves and  moving up and down on his penis using your thighs. (It's a great strengthening exercise!) If you sit up nice and tall and keep your shoulders back, it flattens your tummy by elongating the stomach muscles and gives him a great view of your breasts as you move up and down.

Try the **missionary** position with you on your back and him facing you if you want to keep your lower half out of sight, including your butt and your thighs. You can even wrap your thighs around him. That way they are right behind him.  He'll be able to see your breasts and part of your tummy if he's up on his knees, but mostly he'll be looking at your face so it's very intimate without being fully on display.

**Spooning** is not much of a visual treat for your guy (which he might not like). In this position, you lie on your side facing away from your guy and he lies nestled behind you. He can't see any of your front at all (or in fact anything but the back of your neck and shoulders). Although it means he can't see any of your body as he enters you from behind, you may actually find it's not very pleasurable hiding yourself (except for an occasional variation) because it's not as intimate as other positions.

**Sixty-nine** (where you give each other oral sex at the same time) is a position where the most he is going to see is between your legs, and he'll be pretty much wrapped up in what he is doing to you as well as what you are doing to him. After a few minutes of that, it's pretty likely that you won't care whatever position you do next and what he sees, and neither will he!

If you a bit overweight and have **sex standing up**, you'll find that even if you are fully naked everything is going to look much better (at least in your mind) than if you are lying down and bending over with your fat going into rolls when you wish it didn't. You know from everything in this book that you should not care about that. In fact, even skinny girls bent over get those rolls. But if you do care, you will like what sex against the wall does for you – not to mention how erotic it can be that the two of you can't wait until you get into bed!

# 33

## Forget The Past

If you have had an embarrassing sexual experience in the past (there must be very few of us who haven't) or if you've had a bad experience from going to bed with a jerk, don't let that get in the way of having a good time now. Put that all behind you.

Reminding yourself of it is like picking at a scar so you can bleed again. Just because something happened in the past that dented your confidence a bit does not mean that you're destined to failure forever. All that counts is the guy you're with now and the fun you can have with him. Imagining a successful outcome over and over is a helpful way to delete the past from your mind and enjoy what you have now (see Strategy 25).

If bedroom bloopers do happen (and they happen to everyone), remember to laugh with your partner. Perfect sex only happens in movies and things do go wrong. Treat any mishaps, noises or embarrassing blunders in a lighthearted way. It's supposed to be fun, not serious. See Strategy 34 for more on this.

# 34

# Know How To Handle
# Tricky Situations

There are some situations you'll encounter in the bedroom
that can easily undermine your confidence if you let them.
But with a little knowledge and a bit of tact and humor, you
can handle just about anything that occurs.

## Should You Fake?

If you don't orgasm during sex, you might wonder whether
you should act as if you did, but you should never fake this. It
doesn't matter how long he has been trying to bring you off

and how much you want to please him by pretending to have an orgasm, faking won't help matters one bit. All you're doing is teaching him how not to give you an orgasm the next time, and the more often you fake, the worse it gets. Have the confidence to be honest about this or you might find yourself months down the line having to confess that you have never had an orgasm with him.

Make sure you know how to give yourself an orgasm before you have sex so you can gently show him how (and you can always give him a helping hand while he massages your breasts or enters you). Being confident enough to take your pleasure in hand (so to speak) is a great asset in bed and will mean you are never left high and dry. He won't mind your help at all, as long as you don't criticize what he is doing and just show him in the spirit of "This is what I like." He would probably enjoy watching you pleasure yourself once you're confident enough to show him.

## Losing Control

It's perfectly fine to get carried away by the moment. Being a control freak in the bedroom is not a good thing. You can let it all out and show that you are really into him and he will love it! You can't go wrong screaming his name or anything else (except the name of another guy!)

## First Time With Him

You'll both be nervous so don't feel like you have to impress him with your entire sexual repertoire. You are at the stage of getting to know each other's bodies and what you like. Either take the whole thing slowly and spend time getting to know what turns him on or have a quickie which will be exciting in itself if you are already turned on (with the idea being that you can't help yourself) before taking things more slowly.

## Asking Him To Wear A Condom

Always have a condom or two with you if sex may be on the cards, and then just ask outright, "Do you have a condom?", so that if he says he doesn't, you can say you have one in your pocket or bag somewhere. Though you may feel awkward about interrupting things or hinting that he may be diseased, you have to do this for your own peace of mind with a new guy. In many ways he should be pleased that you insist on this as he knows that you take care and will be clean too. If he complains about wearing one, then tough. Make it clear if he doesn't, you're out of there. It's not worth the risk.

You can buy condoms online if you're too shy to buy in a store, but it's pretty simple to pop them in your basket along with your other shopping. No one will bat an eyelid.

**110**

## Asking For What You Want

One thing not to do is to tell your guy he's not doing it right. That can deflate his ego (and the parts you don't want to deflate). Let him know when he does something that feels good, and it's fine to say "faster" or "harder". If his hand isn't quite in the right spot, say "a little higher" or move your body to the right position so he is getting it right. Don't worry that he might reject you if you tell him what you want. Whatever you do, he'll be aroused by you taking action and that you were confident enough to show him.

## You're Dry

There is a good chance that are you are not relaxed enough and need more time and more foreplay to get into the swing of things. If you have an ongoing problem with vaginal dryness, use lubricant and check with your doctor.

## You Feel Like Peeing

Many older women release a little urine at the moment of orgasm, in the same way that they might when they cough, laugh unexpectedly or sneeze. The easiest solution is to go to the toilet before you get started. You may also get the urge to pee in some sexual positions but won't normally release any urine - not to be confused with female ejaculate which is clear and odorless and may be released at the time of orgasm.

## You Make a Rude Noise

Air often gets trapped in the vagina during certain sexual positions and makes a noise, like a fart, when it is released. You might even fart for real at the crucial moment. Don't worry, just laugh it off and keep going.

# 35

## Expand Your Confidence Outside The Bedroom

Your guy is not in bed with a body. He is in bed with you – the whole of you. You can't detach a body from a person – you're a whole package.

Build up your self-esteem by remembering who you are and what you stand for, your gifts and values, what you get done, what you do for others, and what you've achieved. Pat yourself on the back whenever you do anything right. Forgive yourself quickly and resolve to learn from your mistakes whenever you're not so happy with your performance.

We are all learning every day of our lives – so give yourself credit for that.

Building up your confidence outside the bedroom will mean you have more self-assurance in all kinds of situations, as well as during sex. Because you have fewer opportunities to practice being confident in bed, you can go a long way faster by doing all you can to increase your confidence in all kinds of ways. Some examples of things you can do to give yourself a general boost are

- Dress well and get rid of all the clothes in your closet that don't make you feel good. Slouching around in faded sweats never made anyone feel sexy. Casual is good. Sloppy is not.

- Learn to smile more often. Not only will you feel better, but you'll make others feel good too, and that will enhance your self-esteem in a subtle way. The friendlier you are, the better you will feel about yourself.

- Get your posture right. Positive body language releases feel good hormones in the body so physiology has a lot to do with general confidence. Slumped, rounded shoulders and looking down at the ground makes you feel low and depressed. If you find yourself slumping, consciously correct your posture, put a bounce in your step and walk tall, and you'll feel much more confident.

- Be a giver. Helping others will make you feel better about yourself and contribute to your overall feeling of self-worth. Even tiny things like holding doors open and giving way in traffic can make you feel good. Bigger gestures, such as helping those who are homeless, will have an even greater effect. You don't need to brag about it, just do it and feel good about it.

- Take pride in your surroundings. Do your best to keep your home or your room looking good or at least clean and tidy, and clear all the trash out of your car too. The more pride you have in small things like this, the more confident you will feel overall.

- Be brave and do things you are a bit scared about in other areas of your life, and that can rub off on how confident you are in other ways – sign up to do a fun run (or a marathon), join a salsa dancing class if you think you have two left feet, or a cookery class if you can't boil an egg, especially if you secretly think you will enjoy these activities if only you were brave enough to go for it. Expand your repertoire of skills and the happier you will be with yourself. The more you do, the more you will build your self-esteem and the more attractive you will appear to yourself and others.

- Have some goals that you are striving for. Goal setting itself gives you a boost in physical and mental energy. And every time you accomplish something that brings you closer to what you want to achieve, you will feel even better about yourself.

- Take responsibility for how your life goes. Make sure you react to anything that happens in a positive way rather than being a victim of circumstances. Bad things happen to everyone, but you can either look at the situation and try and find your way out of it or decide to blame your bad luck for everything wrong in your life and do nothing. Confidence comes from action, not blame.

If you would like more ideas for how to expand your general confidence, pick up the free bonus that comes with this book "How To Be Confident And Feel Happy With Yourself." (Details are in the "FREE for you" section below).

You will feel so much better about every part of your life.

# FINALLY

Congratulations! You've arrived at the final part of this book. You now have 35 strategies to choose from to be more confident and happier with yourself in bed. If you put some of these techniques into practice, you can't help but feel good. Now it's time to choose where you want to start and begin your campaign.

Sometimes the road to confidence is a rocky one, but by taking one step at a time, you will get there. In any case, you'll always be streets ahead of where you would be if you hadn't even started. So don't wait for the perfect time to feel good about yourself. The perfect time is now.

Once you've read to the very end, loop right around to the start of the book and decide on a plan of action. Two or three strategies is a great start.

## What's Next? More Confidence?

This book covered just one aspect of what I call "Captivating Confidence" – feeling SO good about yourself that you can't fail to have more success out there in the world and attract others to you.

"Feel Good Naked" is actually part of a series of guides that help you have more confidence in life, particularly the kind of confidence you need to be happy in love.

When it comes to dating and relationships, confidence is essential. Without a good dose of it, you'll find it difficult to

- enjoy happy long-term relationships as an equal to your partner

- get to know guys you like

- have them recognize you as "the one"

- hold your own when it comes to calling the shots

- move on from guys who don't treat you right

- trust a guy enough to open up so he gets to know you and love you on the deepest level.

The "Captivating Confidence" guides help you have all the confidence you need to create rock-solid relationships whether it's getting to know guys and feeling more confident flirting with them or feeling better about yourself after a breakup so that you're ready to find a new love. There's also help with everything from first dates and kissing to confidently negotiating the world of online dating.

## Out Now: You Are Beautiful!

If feeling good about how you look is a problem all the time and not just when you are naked, pick up a copy of "You Are Beautiful! 53 Easy Ways To Love Your Imperfect Self." The additional strategies in the book will make you feel great about yourself day in and day out, and they will also reinforce everything that yo:u discovered here.

## Coming Soon

- How To Feel Confident After Break-Up And Rejection

- Confident Flirting: Feel Comfortable Around Guys You Like

You can get updates about new releases in the "Captivating Confidence" series when you get your FREE book (details below).

# More Confidence: $9.99 or FREE For You

If you would like to have more self-confidence in every area of your life, pick up a copy of the companion book in this series "Rock-solid Confidence Step By Step: How To Be Confident And Happy With Yourself" It's available in paperback priced at $9.99.

Alternatively, you can download it absolutely FREE with my best wishes, as a thank you for your interest in this book, in exchange for answering one quick question about confidence. Get all the details here:

http://lovefromana.com/moreconfidence

As well as the book, you'll get the latest news and updates from the author including future free reports and useful guides.

# Helpful Books And Websites

## realwomensbodies.com

This website explores the whole topic of body image and has the goal of helping to build a healthy positive image of real women in the world at large and in our own minds.

"Hopefully this site will leave you feeling better about your own body as you begin to see the true beautiful variety of real women's bodies."

## 007b.com

A whole website on loving your breasts just as they are - big, small, pert, sagging, uneven, flat. If you have particular problems accepting this part of your body, take a look. There are hundreds of pictures in galleries of real women's breasts, and after a few minutes browsing there, you will realize that yours are perfect just the way they are, whatever their size and shape.

## abeautifulbodyproject.com

Well worth a look, the Beautiful Body Project is about acceptance of the beauty of the whole female body in all its forms. It is a platform and network of female photographers dedicated to creating therapeutic and truthful photos, videos and stories to help women and girls build self-esteem.

## theshapeofamother.com

This site provides a look at the real bodies of women who have been pregnant. This is a good site for support if you were happy with your body before you had a child and are less happy with it now. Shape Of A Mother is "where we share photos of our bodies before, during and after pregnancy to know we are not alone in the changes that happen to us."

## Dove Videos

Whatever you think about a beauty company trying to promote a healthy body image while still trying to sell products, you have to admire this one for at least recognizing

**124**

the issue. With their "Campaign for Real Beauty," Dove are trying to get women to recognize that beauty comes in many forms - ones that you don't usually find in advertising. And given that their products are simple beauty basics and not the priciest, it's not as if they are pushing products that women don't want or need.

You'll find some great videos on youtube.com. Look for (without quotes) "dove evolution," "dove body evolution," "dove amy" and "dove onslaught." These videos are designed to make you think – and they do.

## Other Books From The Publisher

### Ten Years Younger In A Weekend

Forget Botox, cosmetic surgery, expensive skin creams you can't afford, and punishing regimens. This is a collection of all the things you can do to look good at any age, right now. See *beautytoptotoe.com/ten-years-younger* for details.

### Fitness In No Time

For those who don't have much time but want to be fit and healthy, here is a simple program for beginners you can do in ten minutes three times a week to get fit, strong and supple.

Every body deserves 30 minutes a week. For details see *simplyfitnessgear.com/notime/*

## Walk Your Way To Weight Loss With Your Pedometer

A program which is as much about getting healthy as it is about losing excess pounds. See *walkoffweight.org* for details.

## Excite Diet: Beat Diet Boredom

If you're bored with the same old diets, this book can help motivate you to keep going as you get to choose a new strategy every day and vary them as much as you like to fit in with your lifestyle and plans. See *excitedietbook.com* for all 50 ways to beat diet boredom.

# THANK YOU!

I hope you enjoyed this, the second book in the "Captivating Confidence" series. You're now armed with the strategies you need to feel not just great but fantastic about your naked self.

If you like the book, I'd appreciate it if you could leave a short review where you made your purchase. It will help me improve this and future books and help other women decide if "Feel Good Naked: 35 Secrets Of Irresistible Body Confidence" is right for them too.

Let's spread the message far and wide that real women are beautiful just as they are.

# About the Author

Like many women these days, Ana Wilde is a full-time juggler of multiple roles. She is a writer, publisher, and the owner of a small business. She lives with her husband and two kids in an old house in Scotland, where she is chief cook and bottle washer as well as finder of all lost things. Find Ana online at *LoveFromAna.com*.

## Other Books By Ana

182 Great Places to Meet Men: Get The Guy You Want

PLAY! 77 Sexy Games For Two To Spice Up Your Love Life

### *In The Captivating Confidence Series*

You Are Beautiful! 53 Easy Ways To Love Your Imperfect Self

## Contact The Author

Feedback, questions and comments are welcome via email. I'd love to hear from you. You can get in touch with me at any time via my email address ana@lovefromana.com.

Love from

Ana

P.S. You're welcome to join in the fun by commenting and sharing here too:

Blog:          http://lovefromana.com

Twitter:       https://twitter.com/lvfromana

Facebook:   https://www.facebook.com/lovefromana

## Join The Love From Ana Reader Panel

If you liked this book and want to be part of the reader panel who review pre-release copies of future books, please send me an email at ana@lovefromana.com mentioning you would like to take part and I will be in touch.

Made in the USA
San Bernardino, CA
17 July 2015